Thank you for inviting these lovable creatures into your artistic realm. May your days be as bright as the hues you choose, and may this book bring warmth and smiles to your heart.

With heartfelt appreciation,

Rafael Migliorini

2023

This Book Belongs to:

Test Color Page